AUSSIE SLANG DICTIONARY

Published by Brolga Publishing Pty Ltd
ABN 46 063 962 443
PO Box 12544
A'Beckett St
Melbourne, VIC, 8006
Australia
sales@brolgapublishing.com.au

Copyright © Lolla Stewart 2011

All rights reserved. No part of this publication may be reproduced, stored in a
retrieval system, or transmitted in any form or by any means, electronic, mechanical,
photocopying, recording or otherwise, without the prior permission of the Publisher.

National Library of Australia Cataloguing-in-Publication entry

Aussie slang dictionary : easy guide to Aussie slang /
compiled by Lolla Stewart.
8th ed.
9781922036308 (pbk.)
English language – Australia – Slang – Dictionaries.
427.994

Printed in China
Cover design by David Khan
Typeset by Imogen Stubbs
New quotes for updated editions collated by Christine Fotis

AUSSIE SLANG DICTIONARY

An easy guide to Aussie slang

Compiled by Lolla Stewart

A

A bit more choke and you would have started: said to somebody who has just passed wind loudly.

A over T: short for arse over tit, meaning upside down or head over heels.

Ace: excellent.

Acid: the good word: the truth. *The good acid.*

Ac/dc: bisexual.

Act the goat: to behave foolishly.

Adam's ale: water.

Add insult to injury: to make matters even worse than they already are.

Aerial ping-pong: Australian Rules Football. A reference to the spectacular leaps which players can make to 'mark' the ball.

After dark: rhyming slang for shark. *Watch out for the after dark.*

Aggro: aggressive. *He got aggro with me.* Also used as a noun: *she was really givin' me the aggro.*

Airy fairy: vague.

Akubra: broad-brimmed Aussie hat made out of pressed rabbit fur and worn by farmers and famous golfers!

Alf: stupid person.

Alice, The: Alice Springs, Northern Territory town near Uluru (Ayers Rock).

Alley up: to pay back a debt.

All froth and no beer: superficial, without substance.

Alligator: a horse.

Alligator pear: avocado. Named for

the reptile like skin of the fruit and the pear like shape.

All over him/her like a rash: refers to a person who can't keep their hands to themselves.

All over red rover: completely finished.

All over the place like a mad woman's breakfast: a mess; in a state of chaos.

All wool and a yard wide: authentic; trustworthy.

All your Christmases have come at once: a bonus of good luck.

Alone like a country dunny: alone; lonely; abandoned.

Amber fluid: beer.

Ambo: ambulance or ambulance driver.

Anchors: brakes of a vehicle.

Angle of the dangle: the state of an erection.

Aussie Slang Dictionary

Ankle-biter: a toddler; small child.

Ants pants: looking good, similar to *the bees knees.*

Anyhow mate: a saying used to change the subject of a conversation, or signal leaving due to boredom.

Any tick of the clock: very soon, any time now.

ANZAC: acronym for Australian and New Zealand Army Corp. Refers to WWWI soldiers (called diggers) who were the first ANZACs, and generally to Australian soldiers.

Apeshit: to express extreme anger. *The boss went apeshit when I arrived late.*

Apples (she'll be): everything will work out okay.

Apple eaters: refers to someone who lives or is from Tasmania (apple growing state).

Apple Isle: Tasmania.

A

Argie-bargie: testy; argumentative.

Argue the toss: to question a decision. *There's no point arguing the toss with me, son.*

Around the twist: insane.

Arse about face: back to front.

Arse around: to fool around; to muck about; to waste time.

Arse off: to depart; to leave.

Arse over tit: trip or fall over.

Arvo: afternoon.

Aussie: shortened form of Australia/Australian.

Aussie battler: an ordinary Australian trying to make ends meet.

Aussie salute: brushing flies away from the face with your hand.

Australian as meat pie: authentic.

Autumn leaf: a jockey who continually falls off.

Avago: have-a-go. To attempt or try to do something.

Away with the pixies/birds: day dreaming; in another world.

Awning over the toy shop: male beer belly, with the toy shop referring to the genitals.

Axle grease: money.

Ay: hey, hello or used to signal when you haven't understood what someone is saying.

B

Baccy: tobacco.

Back blocks (out in the): beyond suburbia and the more established farm and cattle properties.

Backchat: to answer impertinently a person in authority, or parent.

Back door bandit: uncomplimentary term for a homosexual male.

Backhander: a bribe; underhand payment.

Back o' Bourke: outback; remote country area.

Back of beyond: outback Australia.

Bad case of the trots: diarrhoea.

Bag: an ugly woman or to criticise

Aussie Slang Dictionary

something, similar to *knock*.

Bagman: swagman; tramp; drifter.

Bagman's gazette: mythical source of bush rumours.

Bag of fruit: rhyming slang for suit.

Bail out: to leave.

Bail up: to hold up, rob, earbash or confront someone.

Bald as a bandicoot: having no hair.

Ball and chain: the wife as referred to in her absence.

Balls: testicles.

Balls-up: used when something goes terribly wrong. *The club awards night was a complete balls-up.* The reference is to testicles, not toys!

Bananas: to be crazy with anger. *Shazza went bananas the other night when I told her about the car.*

Banana-bender: Queenslander.

Bangs like a dunny door in a gale: refers to a woman free with sexual favours. Also see "D" for dunny.

Bang on: to hit the target right in the middle, right/correct.

Banged up: pregnant.

Banjo: frying pan; shoulder of mutton.

Barbie: barbeque.

Barcoo buster: outback Queensland term for a wind from the west.

Bar flies: (old) men who hang around the pub all day.

Bark at the lawn: to vomit. *Let me through, fellas! I gotta go bark at the lawn.*

Barmy as a bandicoot: insane.

Barney (to have a): fight, scuffle or argument.

Barrack for: to support a sports team, or player. *I barrack for the Kangaroos.*

Bastard: can be used in both a positive and negative way. *He was a real bastard!* Or *Long time no see, you old bastard!*

Bash: noun for a wild party; verb to punch, to attack someone or something. *He bashed the livin' daylights out of it.* Also *she gave me a real ear bashing.* Meaning she nagged or scolded.

Basket case: hopeless, emotionally broken. *After he lost his job he became a real basket case.*

Bastard from the bush: a country boy, a yokel.

Bat: an ugly woman.

Bathers: swimming costume.

Bats: crazy; insane.

Battery acid: cheap white cask wine, tastes like vinegar.

Battler: usually referred to as *the little Aussie battler:* an individual struggling against the odds to make a better life, but never getting ahead.

Bazza: nickname for Barry. Also a general term for the Aussie bloke. Names such as Garry, Darren, Sharon, are shortened in a similar way to Gazza, Dazza, Shazza.

Bazzaland: Australia.

Beanie: close fitting woollen knitted hat.

Beak: magistrate, judge or your nose.

Bearded clam: a description of the female genitals.

Beat around the bush: to go around the topic, avoid the point in question.

Beaten by a blow: shearer slang referring to the running of shears from one end of a sheep to the other.

Beaut, beauty : great, excellent.

Beer gut: bulging or fat stomach.

Beer o'clock: the end of the work day when you go to the pub for a beer.

Bee's dick: smallest possible margin. *He won by a bee's dick.* Or *you've got a bee's dick chance of winning, mate.*

Bee's knees: the best.

Beg yours?: pardon me?.

Belly-buster, belly/whacker: stomach-first dive in water. Ouch!

Belly-up: refers to the failure of a venture or enterprise or death.

Belt: to hit or punch.

Belt up: stop talking, be quiet.

Belyando spew: shearer's illness, usually associated with poor cooking conditions.

Bend the elbow: to drink a bit too much. He bends the elbow a bit doesn't he?

Bender: a drinking spree.

Bent as a scrub tick: crazy; foolish.

Berko: furious, mad. *She went berko at me.*

Better half: the spouse. *Dave, meet my better half.*

Better than a poke in the eye with a burnt stick: not as bad as the alternative; an admission that things could be worse.

Bewdy: similar to beaut. Means very good or excellent. *You got the beer? Bewdy!*

Bible-basher: over enthusiastic evangelical Christian.

Big bickies: a large amount of money.

Big note oneself: to boast or brag.

Big smoke: the city.

Big sticks: the goal posts in Aussie Rules football.

Bike (the town): a reference to a promiscuous woman.

Bikkie/bickie: biscuit.

Billabong: a waterhole.

Billiard ball (as sharp as a): not perceptive, mentally slow.

Billy: tin container with handle for boiling water over a campfire.

Billy Bluegum: a koala.

Billy cart: a go-kart, often homemade for children to use.

Billy lids: rhyming slang for kids.

Billyo: fast, with great speed. *He took off like billyo with the dog chasing him.*

Bin: prison; gaol.

Bindy: grass burr or nettle.

Binge: like a bender, a drinking spree.

Bingle: a minor car accident.

Biscuit: cookie.

Bite on (to put the): ask/pressure someone for money.

Bite your bum: shut up; get lost.

Bities: collective term for insects that bite, ie. spiders, bull ants.

Aussie Slang Dictionary

Bit more choke and your would have started (a): refers to a person who has just farted loudly.

Bitser: a dog of mixed parentage, a mongrel. Refers to *bits of this, bits of that.*

Bizzo: business. *Mind your own bizzo.*

Black stump: a mythical place that signifies the edge of the outback. *The road goes way beyond the Black Stump.*

Bleeder: man (derogatory term).

Bleeding oath: expression of unqualified agreement.

Blimey: an expression of surprise. *Blimey! Did you see that 'roo?*

Blind Freddie: mythical person representing the lowest common denominator in comprehension skills. *The punchline was so obvious, Blind Freddie could have seen it coming.*

Bloke: a man. Generally a positive label.

Bloodhouse: a rough pub.

Blood'n'blister: sister (rhyming slang).

Blood's worth bottling: refers to a person of uniquely admirable qualities.

Bloody: the great Australian adjective in widespread use. Serves to emphasise the word that follows it. *Bloody good! Bloody awful! Bloody hell! It's about bloody time!*

Bloody oath: an agreement. *Will we strike? Bloody oath we will!*

Blotto: blind drunk.

Blow a fuse: to lose one's temper.

Aussie Slang Dictionary

Blow in the bag: to take a breathalyser test.

Blower: the telephone.

Blowie: blow fly, the large, droning kind.

Blow-in: an uninvited guest.

Blow through: leave in a hurry.

Bludge: to sponge off someone or the system.

Bludger: a person who doesn't make an effort but takes something for nothing.

Blue: a fight or an argument or a red-headed person.

Blue (make a): make a mistake.

Blue duck: disappointment; mistake.

Blue-flier: a fast kangaroo.

Blue Heeler: the police or a breed of dog.

Blue-nosed wowser: killjoy; party-pooper; teatotaller (non-drinker); someone who kills the mood or ruins a party.

Blues: the police.

Bluestone college: Pentridge Prison.

Blue-tongue: shearer's term for a shed hand – an unskilled worker.

Bluey: a swag, a rolled up blanket OR an infringement notice issue by the police.

Bobby dazzler: someone or something excellent.

Bob's worth/two bob's worth: opinion; point of view.

Bob's your uncle: a summary way of expressing that things are, or will be, fine. *We'll bring the booze, your bring the food, we'll meet at the beach and Bob's your uncle.*

Bodgy: of inferior quality.

Bog: the toilet. Also to defacate.

Bogan: cultural sub-group who listen to old rock music, generally own pit bull terriers and have late-eighties haircuts. A rough type of individual.

Bogged: stuck car, usually in mud or sand.

Bog house: toilet.

Bog in: to commence eating.

Bog roll: toilet paper.

Bog standard: basic; unadorned; without accessories.

Boiler: an older woman. Refers to hens too old to roast.

Boil the billy: to put the kettle on; to make a hot drink.

Bolted: to leave quickly, run off.

Bomb: a car that hardly goes, is rusted out, or is covered in dints and scratches.

Bondi cigar: a turd floating in the sea.

Bondi tram: usually *to shoot through like a Bondi tram:* to leave in a hurry, often leaving unpaid debts.

Bonkers: insane, crazy.

Bonza: top quality, excellent.

Booby: a foolish person.

Boogie board: half size surfboard.

Bookie: bookmaker.

Boomer: kangaroo; or anything excessively large.

Boomerang: a dishonoured cheque – it bounces back.

Boots'n'all: wholeheartedly; all in.

Booze artist: heavy drinker.

Booze bus: mobile police breathalysing station.

Boozer: the local pub or an individual who drinks at the same.

Booze-up: a party with more alcohol than food.

Bo-peep (to go for a): to take a sly look at something that isn't your business.

Bore the pants off (someone): to be excessively boring.

Bot: to scab, to bludge off, borrow with no intention of giving back. *Can I bot a cigarette of ya, mate?*

B

Botfly: a scrounger; a scab; someone who is always taking but never giving.

Bottle shop/Bottle-O: liquor store, usually attached to a pub.

Bottler: an individual or experience of remarkable quality. Refers to the desire to capture and keep it in a bottle.

Bottom-of-the-harbour scheme: a tax dodge.

Bounce: bully.

Bowerbird: a compulsive hoarder.

Bow wow: really ugly.

Boys in blue: police.

Bradman: sporting opponent who is unbeatable. A reference to the unequalled cricketer, Sir Donald Bradman.

Brain bucket: bicycle safety helmet.

Brazz monkey weather: very cold.

Aussie Slang Dictionary

Brass razoo: a negative term meaning having no money. *Don't look at me, mate, I haven't got a brass razoo.*

Breadbasket: stomach.

Break open a coldie/tinnie: to open a beer.

Breakfast bird: a kookaburra.

Breather: a rest. *Let's take a breather, fellas.*

Breeze: an easy task.

Brekkie: breakfast.

Brickie: bricklayer.

Brick short of a load: simple-minded; stupid.

Bride's nightie (up and down like a): referring to something that fluctuates.

Bright as a two watt globe: not very bright person; stupid; dumb.

Bright-eyed and bushy-tailed: describes a person who is in good health and spirits and is rearing to get started on something.

Bright spark: clever; intelligent.

Brizzie/Brisvegas: Brisbane.

Broad in the beam: having large hips and/or bottom.

Broken packet of biscuits (he's a): something or someone who looks good on the outside, but is a mess on the inside.

Brown eye: to show ones bottom, mooning.

Brown-eyed mullet: a poo floating in the sea.

Brown nose: to ingratiate oneself, to fawn, or *crawl*.

Bruce: a general name for a man.

Brumby: wild horse in the bush.

Aussie Slang Dictionary

Brummy: counterfeit; dud.

Bubbler: a drinking fountain.

Buckley's: a slim chance, or none at all. *You've got Buckley's, love*.

Budgie smugglers: men's swimming costume. Also known by the brand Speedo.

Buffer: an elderly man.

Buffin' the muffin: sexual intercourse.

Bugger: widespread expression of disappointment. *Oh, bugger!* OR a term similar to bastard and used in both positive and negative ways. *Come here, you old bugger, and give us a hug*.

Bugger-all: nothing or very little.

Bugger off: to shoot through, leave.

Buggered: exhausted, worn out.

Buggered if I know: to have no idea or

26

know nothing about something.

Buggerlugs: irreverent, but also affectionate name for someone. *Buggerlugs here wants to go home.*

Buggery: mythical place, a long way away, reserved for those whom we tell to bugger off. *He can go to buggery for all I care.*

Bugle: a nose. *That dead fish was a bit on the bugle.*

Built like a brick shit house: someone or something strong.

Bullamakanka: mythical place in the outback.

Bull bar: metal bar fixed to the front of a vehicle (typically a 4WD) to protect it from hitting kangaroos. Also known as a *roo bar.*

Bull dust: a lie.

Bull's wool: misleading information.

Aussie Slang Dictionary

Bully for you: derisive exclamation.

Bum: backside, bottom.

Bum fluff: adolescent's first growth of facial hair.

Bum nuts: eggs.

Bummer: a let-down or disappointment.

Bundy: Bundaberg rum.

Bun in the oven: pregnant.

Bunch of fives: a fist. The same thing as a knuckle sandwich.

Bung: broken, not working or to place something carelessly. *Just bung it over there.*

Bung it on/bung on an act: to act with attitude.

Bunyip: a mythical Aboriginal bush spirit animal that lives in swamps and billabongs.

28

Burl: to attempt something. *I'll give it a burl.*

Burl along: to hurtle along; to keep going regardless.

Burr up: get angry.

Bush: the countryside; any rural area.

Bush baptist: a heavily religious person.

Bush bash: to go off road in a vehicle, forcing your way through untouched bush.

Bush carpenter: self-taught carpenter or tradesman whose work is slap-happy or crude.

Bush dinner: damper and black tea.

Bushed: exhausted; lost; tired.

Bushfire blonde: a redheaded person.

Bushie (also bushwhacker): farmer or country dweller of straightforward nature.

Aussie Slang Dictionary

Bushman's clock: a kookaburra.

Bushman's hot dinner: damper and mustard.

Bush oyster: nasal mucus.

Bush pig: an unattractive person.

Bushranger: outlaw; thief of the bush; outback criminal.

Bush telegraph: gossip; grapevine.

Bush telly: campfire.

Bushweek: a fictional time when everybody slacks off and everything goes wrong. *Hurry up, you lot. What do you think this is, bushweek?*

Bushytailed: full of health and good spirits; awake bright and early in the morning.

Busy as a centipede on a hotplate: very busy.

30

Busy as a one legged bloke in an arse kicking contest: to be doing nothing.

Butcher's/butcher's hook: from rhyming slang meaning a look. *Take a butcher's hook at that poor bastard.*

Butcher's canary: fly (insect).

Butterfly: a coin that fails to spin when tossed.

B.Y.O.: bring your own alcohol to a restaurant.

C

Cabbage patcher: resident of Victoria.

Cack-handed: left handed.

Cackleberry: an egg.

Cactus: ruined; no good for anything. *We can't use my car, it's cactus.*

Cakehole: mouth.

Call it a day: the end; to finish what you're doing and go home.

Call 'Ralph': to vomit.

Camp as a row of tents: a homosexual male.

Cancer stick: cigarette.

Cane toad: a Queenslander.

Can't take a trick: describes a person who has a run of bad luck.

Captain Cook: rhyming slang for a look.

Cark it: to die.

Carn!: come on! An encouraging cry to your sports team. *Carn the Bombers!*

Carpet grub: a small child, often at the crawling stage.

Carpet muncher: a lesbian.

Carry on like a pork chop: to behave in a silly manner, or to express frustration or anger out of proportion to the problem.

Carry the mail: to buy drinks, normally at a pub or bar.

Cat's hiss: rhyming slang for piss.

Cat's pyjamas: refers to a person who thinks they're better than others. *He thinks he's the cat's pyjamas.*

Aussie Slang Dictionary

Caustic crackers and strawberry sand: to have marriage and/or relationship problems.

Chalkie: teacher.

Charge like a wounded bull: to ask ridiculously high prices.

Charge like the light brigade: same as above, very expensive fee structure.

Chateau de cardboard: cask of wine.

Cheap as chips: inexpensive.

Cheap drunk: someone who becomes drunk quickly, normally only after one or two drinks.

Cheapskate: unwilling to spend money.

Cheerio: goodbye.

Cheese and kisses: rhyming slang for the missus; the wife.

Chew and spew: a cheap cafe.

Chew the fat: to have a good chat.

34

C

Chewie: chewing gum.

Chewie on your boot!: an Australian Rules Football cat-call inciting the player to miss when going for a goal.

Chiak: to tease, pour scorn on or generally muck about.

China plate: rhyming slang for mate.

Chinwag: gossip, natter.

Chippie: a carpenter.

Chockers, chock-a-block: as full as is possible. *I couldn't eat another thing. I'm chockers.*

Chokkie: chocolate.

Choof off: to leave.

Chook: a hen; a chicken.

Chook house: chicken pen.

Choom: an Englishman.

Chop (not much): expresses disappointment in something. *The weather's not much chop today, eh?*

Choppers: teeth; dentures.

Chrome dome: a bald man.

Chromo: a prostitute.

Chuck a sickie: calling in sick to work when you're not sick.

Chuck a U-ie: execute a u-turn.

Chuck up: to vomit.

Chuck a wobbly or spaz: to throw a temper tantrum.

Chunder: vomit.

Chunderous: nauseating.

Clackers: teeth.

Clagged out: worn out; dead

Clagged the bag: worn out; dead.

C

Clanger: a 'faux pas'; a conversation stopper. *She dropped a clanger when she asked how much it cost.*

Clayton's: a substitute; not the real thing.

Cleanskin: an unlabelled bottle of wine, generally of not-bad quality. Also refers to cattle that have not been branded.

Click: kilometre. *It's 10 clicks away.*

Climb the wall: to go mad.

Clinah/cliner: girlfriend; woman.

Clobber: clothing; to hit hard. *She clobbered him one.*

Clodhoppers: feet.

Clucky: experiencing maternal urges.

Clued up: well informed.

Cluey: smart, knowledgeable.

Aussie Slang Dictionary

Clumsy as a duck in a ploughed paddock: very clumsy; crude; inelegant.

Coathanger, the: Sydney Harbour Bridge.

Cobber: mate.

Cobbler: last sheep to be shorn.

Cock and bull: something that is a lie. *He told me it was free, what a cock and bull.*

Cockatoo: a person posted to keep lookout during illegal activities.

Cockatoo weather: fine by day, rain at night.

Cocky: farmer.

Cocky's joy: golden syrup (similar to maple syrup).

Cockroach: a person from New South Wales.

Codger: an old man.

38

C

Codswallop: rubbish; a lot of nonsense.

Coffin nail: a cigarette.

Cold and dark as a bushman's grave: very cold and gloomy.

Cold as a mother-in-law's kiss: very cold or unwelcoming.

Coldie: chilled beer.

Colonial oath!: an emphatic agreement.

Come a cropper: fall flat on one's face.

Come a gutser: to make a mistake; to have an accident.

Come in spinner!: call during a betting game of two-up.

Comic guts: rhyming slang for stomach or guts.

Compo: workers' compensation.

Conchie: someone who is conscientious.

Cooee: bush call, especially when lost; also means the distance covered by the call. *There isn't a tree within cooee of here.*

Cook: a wife.

Cook the books: fiddle with the accounts in a business; falsify the figures

Coolgardie safe: early form of refrigeration, where foodstuffs were kept cool inside a wooden frame covered with wet hessian. Named after a Western Australian mining town.

Coot: short for bandicoot, usually refers to someone unlikeable.

Cop: to be on the receiving end of something. *He copped a belting from his dad.*

Coppertail: an ordinary person.

Cop shop: police station.

Cop it sweet: to take punishment like a

C

man; to enjoy good fortune.

Corker: excellent; big. *The fish I caught was a corker.*

Cornstalk: a person from New South Wales.

Corroboree: Aboriginal ritual dance.

Cot case: very ill; highly intoxicated; bed ridden.

Cotton on: to understand; to pick up the meaning of something.

Cough drop: idiot.

Could eat a horse and chase the rider: very hungry.

Could kick the arse off an emu: in very good health.

Couldn't fight his way out of a paper bag: refers to a weak or inept person.

Couldn't get a kick in a stampede: said of a poorly performing football player.

Couldn't give a continental: denotes lack of concern.

Couldn't give away cheese at a rats' picnic: utterly hopeless.

Couldn't hit the side of a barn: someone with poor aim.

Couldn't knock the skin off a rice pudding: physically weak; ineffectual.

Couldn't lie straight in bed: refers to a crooked or devious person.

Couldn't organise a screw in a brothel: refers to an inept individual.

Couldn't run a chook raffle in a country pub: thoroughly incompetent; someone with no organisational skills.

Couldn't win if he started the night before: a slow racehorse/individual.

Could sell boomerangs to the Aboriginals: Australian take on *could sell ice to the Eskimos* – very persuasive.

C

Counter lunch/Countery: lunch from a pub.

Country cousin: rhyming slang for a dozen.

Couple of pies short of a grand-final: not all there; mentally deficient.

Cow cockie: dairy farmer.

Cow juice: milk from a cow.

Cows come home (waiting 'til the): waiting all day.

Cozzie: swimming costume.

Crack a fat: to get an erection.

Crack onto (someone): to hit on someone; to pursue romantically.

Cranky: in a bad mood.

Crap: excrement; shit.

Crapper: the toilet.

Crash hot: first rate; excellent; very good.

Crawler: a sycophant; a person trying to gain favours.

Creeping Jesus: an evangelical Christian.

Cripes/crikey: exclamation.

Croak/croak it: to die.

Crock: lies.

Crockery: teeth.

Crocodile: a horse.

Crook: a felon; ill. *The cops caught the*

C

crook. I feel real crook today.

Crooked as a dog's hind leg: devious individual; a line that isn't straight as it should be.

Crow-eater: someone who lives in South Australia.

Crown jewels: male genitalia.

Cruddy: something of low quality.

Crumb gatherer: an AFL player who is good at getting the loose ball.

Crumblies: frail old people.

Crust: job or income. *What do you do for a crust?*

Cubby house: small, timber house in the garden for children to play in.

Cultural cringe: national inferiority complex regarding Aussie artistic accomplishments when compared to the rest of the world.

Cuppa: cup of tea or coffee.

Curly: nickname for a bald person.

Curry (give someone a bit of): give someone a hard time.

Cush: fair and square.

Cushy: a soft and well rewarded job.

Cut lunch: sandwiches.

Cut lunch commando: army reservist.

Cut snake (mad as a): someone so upset they could do anything.

D

Dad'n'Dave: rhyming slang for shave.

Dag: a person of an eccentric or amusing nature; a scruffy individual.

Daggy: unfashionable.

Daisy cutter: term for a ball that is thrown or kicked very low.

Daks: trousers or underpants.

Damage: cost; amount owed. *What's the damage for the meal?*

Damper: bushman's bread made from flour, water and salt.

Dander: rhyming slang for anger.

Dark on: to be angry about something.

Darling shower: dust storm.

Darwin pyjamas: no pyjamas.

Darwin stubby: a very large bottle of beer.

Date: arse, bottom, behind. *Get off your fat date.*

Dead as mutton chops: dead.

Dead but won't lie down: a persistent person.

Dead dingo's donger (as dry as a): very dry.

Dead horse: rhyming slang for sauce; a defunct cause or argument. *I think you're trying to flog a dead horse, mate. Give up!*

Dead marine: empty beer bottle.

Deadset: without a doubt.

Dead sinker: a long glass of beer.

Dead to the world: in a deep sleep, commonly alcohol induced.

Deener: shilling (a pre-decimal coin).

Dekko: a look.

Derro: a down and out person; a homeless person.

Dick head: idiot.

Dicky: of doubtful qualities; risky.

Diddle: to swindle.

Didn't bat an eyelid: showed no emotion; gave no reaction.

Didn't come down in the last shower: shrewd; quick witted.

Digger: gold miner or ANZAC (serviceman).

Digs (your): your house.

Dill: idiot.

Dilly: dotty; idiotic.

Dilly-bag: a food bag or a small bag to carry things.

Aussie Slang Dictionary

Dingaling/dingbat: foolish individual.

Dingdong: a foolish person; noisy argument.

Dingo's breakfast: a yawn, a leak and a good look around.

Dingy: a small aluminium boat.

Dink/double dink: to take a second person on a bicycle. *C'mon, I'll dink ya.*

Dinkum: genuine; authentic.

Dinkum oil: inside information; true.

Dinky di: authentic; real.

Dip out: to fail or withdraw.

Dipstick: an idiot.

Dish licker: dog.

Dishy: glamorous.

Divvy up: to divide; to separate into lots.

Divvy van: police wagon.

Do a flit: to run away or escape responsibility.

Do a Melba: to continually return from retirement.

Do a perish: to die.

Do me a favour: a remark that indicates you want another person to stop making comments.

Do the dirty: to do the wrong thing by someone.

Do your block: to lose your temper.

Do your dash: to reach one's limit.

Do your lolly/na-na/nut: to lose your temper.

Dob: to inform upon someone; to tittle-tattle.

Dobber: one who informs upon others, generally held in contempt.

Aussie Slang Dictionary

Doco: documentary.

Docket: bill; receipt.

Doesn't give a bugger: couldn't care less.

Doesn't know if he's/she's Arthur or Martha: someone who is stupid or in a state of confusion.

Doesn't miss a trick: a very alert person.

Dog and bone: telephone.

Dog box: an old fashioned train with no corridors.

Dog's breakfast: chaos; a mess.
It was all over the place like a dog's breakfast.

Dog's eye: rhyming slang for meat pie.

Dole bludger: somebody on social/ government assistance when unjustified.

Done deal: something that is done or finished.

D

Done like a dinner: thoroughly defeated.

Dong: to strike someone.

Donger: penis.

Donk: motor car engine.

Donkey's years: a very long time.

Don't come the raw prawn: don't try to con or fool me.

Don't do anything I wouldn't do: joking advice to someone going somewhere.

Don't pick your nose or your head will cave in: contemptuous advice to a

53

person exhibiting a complete lack of brains.

Dooks: fists.

Doona: duvet, eiderdown or comforter.

Dosh: money.

Doss-house: boarding house.

Down the hatch!: a popular drinking toast.

Down Under: Australia.

Dial: face.

Drag the chain: to slip behind in a drinking contest.

Draw the crabs: to attract unwelcome attention.

Dribs and drabs: bit by bit. *The school kids arrived in dribs and drabs.*

Drip: stupid individual. *Don't be a drip.*

D

Drippy: boring.

Drink with the flies: to drink alone.

Drive the porcelain bus: to vomit into the toilet bowl.

Drives uphill with the clutch slipping: someone stupid.

Drongo: a real idiot. Refers to a racehorse of the same name who was famous for running last.

Droob: slow witted person, similar to nong, drongo and drip.

Drop a clanger: to make a social blunder or say something inappropriate.

Drop-bears: mythical creatures which fall from trees onto tents at night – a tale to scare young campers.

Drop-kick: a slow-witted individual. *He's a real drop kick, that one.*

Drop off!: go away.

Drop your bundle: to lose control, to have a nervous breakdown.

Drop your guts: to fart/pass wind.

Drover's dog: disparaging reference to the lowest common denominator in capabilities. *It was so easy a drover's dog could have done it.*

Drown some worms: to go fishing.

Drum: information; tip-off. *I'll give you the drum.*

Dry as a dead dingo's donger: very dry or thirsty.

Dry as dog biscuits: something that is very dry and unpleasant to eat.

Dubbo: a country bumpkin.

Duchess: sideboard.

Ducks and drakes: rhyming slang for snakes.

Ducks and geese: rhyming slang for police.

Duck's dinner: a drink of water without anything to eat.

Duck's disease: having a long body but short legs.

Duck shoving: pushing into a queue; dodgy business practice.

Dudder: con-man.

Dud-dropper: someone who sells cheap stuff as good stuff because it is stolen.

Duds: trousers.

Duffer: silly. An affectionate term.

Dull as a month of Sundays: extremely boring.

Aussie Slang Dictionary

Dummy (to spit the): to get very upset.

Dumper: a wave that breaks suddenly on top of surfers and swimmers.

Dunga: angry.

Dunking: dipping a biscuit into a cup of tea or coffee.

Dunlop cheque: a cheque that bounced. Refers to a famous rubber company.

Dunny: a toilet, especially an outdoor one.

Dunny brush: a 'flat top' haircut.

Dunny budgie: fly (insect).

Dunny diver: a plumber.

Dunny rat (cunning as a): a very sly individual.

Durry: cigarette; tobacco.

Dusting: trashing; beating.

Dust-up: a brawl or fight.

E

Ear-basher: someone who talks and talks; a bore.

Earwig: to eavesdrop.

Easy as pushing shit uphill with a toothpick: extremely difficult if not impossible.

Easy as spearing an eel with a spoon: extremely difficult.

Eat the crutch out of a low-flying duck (could): a description of hunger.

Eau de cologne: rhyming slang for telephone.

Egg beater: helicopter.

Egg boiler: bowler hat.

El cheapo: something that is cheap and nasty; a cost cutting individual.

Aussie Slang Dictionary

Elephant's trunk: rhyming slang for drunk.

Emma chisit: how much is it? What does it cost?

Emu parade: a rubbish collecting activity organised in school grounds.

Enzed: New Zealand.

Esky: a portable ice cooler.

Even stevens: equal chance or amount.

Every bastard and his dog: absolutely everybody.

Evo: evening.

Expeno: expensive.

Eyes on, hands off: alright to look, not ok to touch.

60

F

Face fungus: facial hair, ie. a beard or moustache.

Face like a chook's arse: a miserable expression.

Fag: cigarette.

Fair cow: a really annoying person or event.

Fair crack of the whip!: give me a fair go.

Fair dinkum: an exclamation of disbelief or surprise.

Fair go mate: statement you make when someone is not letting you do or say something.

Fair suck of the sauce: a call for even handedness. *Fair suck of the sauce, mate, let the kid have a go.*

Fairy: male homosexual.

Fairy bower: rhyming slang for shower.

Fang carpenter: dentist.

Far gone: beyond repair; madly in love; drunk.

Farmer Giles: rhyming slang for piles; haemorrhoids.

Fat chance: when someone has little or no chance of happening.

Feed the chooks: to submit to a barrage of reporters and TV cameras and give out information.

Feral: a hippie or something disgusting.

Few stubbies short of a six pack: lacking in intelligence.

Fibber: a teller of lies.

Figjam: acronym for *F*** I'm Good, Just Ask Me.* A person who has a high opinion of themselves.

Fit as a mallee bull: in good health, strong.

Five finger discount: shoplifting.

Fizzer: something that peters out or doesn't meet expectations.

Flat out like a lizard drinking: working extremely hard; very busy.

Flake: shark meat for sale in a fish and chip shop.

Flake out: to collape from exhaustion or intoxication.

Aussie Slang Dictionary

Flaming thing/flaming good time: extra bad or extra good.

Flash as a rat with a gold tooth: over dressed.

Flat chat: really busy.

Flat out like a lizard drinking: doing something very fast.

Flat to the boards: extremely busy; working non-stop.

Flemington confetti: rubbish.

Flick: to give something, or someone the flick means to get rid of them in an abrupt manner.

Flicks: the movies.

Flip your lid: to get angry.

Floater: meat pie in a bowl of green pea soup and/or gravy (South Australian delicacy!); a turd.

Flog: to sell something or to steal the

same item! Can also mean to beat another sports team hands down.

Flog the cat: to indulge in self pity.

Flog the log: to masturbate.

Flophouse: accommodation for homeless people.

Flounder spearer: musical conductor (orchestra).

Flu bog: jam.

Fluff: to make a minor error; to fart.

Flutter: a small bet.

Flying the Aussie flag: to be out in public with your shirt tails untucked and hanging loose.

Flynn (in like): to go into something (especially seducing women) with great enthusiasm and haste. Refers to early Australian movie actor, Errol Flynn.

Fly wire: gauze flyscreen covering a

window or doorway.

Folding stuff: paper money.

Footy: Australian Rules Football.

For crying out loud: an expression of annoyance.

For fun and fancy to please old Nancy: an expression used to answer the question 'What are you doing?' when you don't want to tell the truth.

Fossick: to look for surface gold.

Fossick around: search a little aimlessly for something.

Four'b two: rhyming slang for Jew.

Four'n twenty: a popular brand of meat pie; an underage girl offering sexual favours. Also refers to four minutes of fun and twenty years of goal.

Fox: a term given to a drinking partner who leaves before they have to buy a round of drinks.

Franger: a condom.

Fred Nerk: your average citizen, John Doe. Similar to Joe Blow.

Free (a): penalty kick awarded in Australian Rules Football.

Freebie: to get something for nothing.

Fremantle doctor: cool breeze that blows into Perth and Fremantle each afternoon.

French letter/Frenchy: a condom.

Fridee: Friday.

Fried eggs: small breasts.

Aussie Slang Dictionary

Frocks: older ladies dresses.

Front: audacity, cheekiness.

Fruit loop/cake: a stupid person.

Fuck truck: a panel van, usually fitted out with speakers and a mattress and proudly owned by a lusty young male. Similar to *Shaggin' Wagon*.

Full as a boot: very drunk.

Full as a goog: overindulged in food; gorged.

Full as a seaside dunny on Boxing day: to have consumed too much alcohol. Refers to the public conveniences on a crowded beach on December 26.

Full as a state school: bloated.

Full of beans: energetic.

Full up to pussy's bow: to have eaten one's fill; bloated.

Fun bags: a woman's breasts.

F

Funny as a fart in a phone box/ elevator: not amusing.

Funny farm: mental institution.

Furphy: a red herring; a false report.

Further back than Walla Walla: way beyond schedule; last by a long way.

G

'G (the): a shortened form of M.C.G which is the shortened form of the Melbourne Cricket Ground.

Gabba (the): nickname for the Brisbane Cricket ground which is in the suburb of Wooloongabba.

Galah: a person behaving like an idiot. The original galah is a pink and grey Australian parrot.

Galah occasion: an event that requires

formal dress.

Galoot: usually called a big galoot. Another variation on the individual behaving badly. Similar to droob, drip and drongo.

Game as a piss ant: extremely brave.

Game as Ned Kelly: bold as brass and a bit of foolhardy. Ned Kelly was a daring bushranger in Victoria's early days.

Gander: a look. *Take a gander at that, will ya.*

Garbo: garbage collector.

Gargle: a drink.

Gasbag: someone who can talk a lot.

Gazunder: a chamber pot (it 'goes under' the bed).

G'day: famous Australian greeting, equivalent to *Hello* or *Hi*.

Gee and tee: a gin and tonic (drink).

Geebung: a native born Australian living in a remote area.

Geek: a look.

Get off your bike: to lose control of your temper.

Get on like a house on fire: to strike up a friendship; to enjoy each other's company.

Get on your goat: to irritate or annoy.

Get the arse: to be fired from a job.

Get the axe: to lose your job.

Get the drift: to comprehend.

Get the Guernsey: to receive an award or recognition.

Get your arse into gear: someone is asking you to get a move along or hurry up; get organised.

Aussie Slang Dictionary

Get your dander up: to become enraged.

Gibber: enormous plains in the outback covered with small pebbles, mostly red in color.

Ginger Meggs: rhyming slang for legs; also the name for someone with red hair.

Gink: a silly person.

Give it a burl: have a go at something.

Give someone Bondi: to beat them up.

Give something the flick: to dispose of it; get rid of it.

Glutton for punishment: someone who goes back for more hard or unpleasant work.

Gobsmacked: surprised; amazed.

Go bush: to take yourself out of circulation, go to ground for a while, not necessarily in the country.

Go crook: to vent your anger.

Go down the gurgler: to fail in a business venture or enterprise.

Godzone: meaning God's own, Australia. This term is also claimed by New Zealanders.

Gob: mouth.

God botherer: religious fanatic. Similar to *Bible basher*.

Go for the doctor: to take action.

Going off: something that is a lot of fun. *The party was going off.*

Aussie Slang Dictionary

Going like hot cakes: something selling fast.

Going to see a man about a dog: said when one does not want to reveal where they are really going.

Going to see a star about a twinkle: going to the toilet.

Go like the clappers: to work or take off very fast.

Go mulga: to go bush.

Gone on someone: in love with that person.

Gone to the dogs: something or somplace that is no longer any good.

Gone troppo: to go mad or to have lost all sense of civilisation after spending too much time in the tropics.

Good as gold: excellent.

Good nick: to be in a good state of repair, or good health.

Good-oh: okay; good; agreement of satisfaction.

Good on ya!: good for you!

Good sort: an attractive person.

Go through like a dose of salts: to work very fast.

Got space to sell between the ears: brainless.

Go two rounds with a revolving door (couldn't): a weak or ineffectual person.

Go walkabout: to go missing.

Gong: denotes something past its usefulness. *The old motor's had the gong.* Refers to a signal of failure in a talent quest.

Grave jumper: someone who takes someone else's job or seat.

Grazier: sheep or cattle farmer.

Aussie Slang Dictionary

Great Australian salute: swipe at flies around one's face.

Green around the gills: easily given to nausea and vomiting.

Greenie: environmentalist.

Gregory Peck: your neck.

Grey ghost: parking inspector.

Grey nurse: rhyming slang for purse.

Grin and chronic: rhyming slang for gin and tonic.

Grizzle/grizzle guts: complaining person.

Grog: alcohol.

Grog on: to drink.

Grommet: junior surfer.

Grot: dirty or untidy.

Ground parrot: a small farmer.

Grouse: fantastic; excellent.

Grub: someone or something dirty.

Grumble bum: an old whinger.

Gub/gubbah: an old Aboriginal term for a white person.

Guffing off: someone who is lazy.

Gully: a small valley.

Gullyraker: a cattle thief.

Gumboot: rubber boots, Wellingtons or a condom.

Gummy: toothless.

Gumpuncher: a dentist.

Gumsucker: someone who lives in Victoria.

Gundabluey: a heavy downpour of rain.

Gunner/gunna: an individual who procrastinates, who is always *gunna* (going to) do something but rarely does.

Gunyah: a humpy (badly built cottage or shed, often made out of found objects).

Gurgler: plughole.

Guzzle: to drink something quickly.

Guzzler: an alcoholic.

Gyp: (pronounced jip) to swindle.

H

Haggle: try to talk the price down.

Hair like a bush pig's arse: wild, unkept hair.

Hair of the dog: drinking more alcohol as a cure for a hangover.

Hairs on ya chest (to put): something you eat or drink that will (supposably) make you more of a man, or something scary.

Handles like a dog on lino: handles badly.

Hang out: spend time together.

Halfback flanker: rhyming slang for wanker. Refers to a playing position in Australian Rules Football.

Half pinter: a small person.

Ham and eggs: rhyming slang for legs.

Handbrake: a term used by a husband when his wife slows him down, usually on shopping trips.

Happy as a bastard on Father's day: depressed; miserable.

Happy as a box full of birds: in high spirits.

Happy as a boxing kangaroo in a fog: very miserable.

Happy as a pig in mud: very happy.

Happy as Larry: very pleased; content.

Hardcase: someone who is close minded.

Has a death adder in his/her pocket: a tight fisted person; a miser.

Has a few palings missing from the fence: simple, not all there or mentally unstable.

Has a Japanese bladder: has to urinate frequently.

Has a snout on (someone): to hold a grudge.

Has white ants in the woodwork: mentally unbalanced.

Hasn't got a bean/cracker: broke.

Hasn't got all four paws on the mouse: slow witted.

Hasn't got an earthly: has no chance or idea.

Hatter: someone who lives alone.

Have a slash: to urinate.

Aussie Slang Dictionary

Have a snort: to have an alcoholic drink.

Have a sticky/sticky beak: to pry.

Haven't got two bob to rub together: broke.

Haven't they fed the dingoes lately: a greeting to an unexpected guest.

Head like a mini with the doors open: to have large or protruding ears.

Head like a robber's dog: very ugly person.

Heaps: a lot. *He had heaps of beer.*

Heart starter: first alcoholic drink of the day.

Heave: to vomit.

Heebie-jeebies/screaming heebie-jeebies: terror; an awful fright.

Hen fruit: eggs.

Hey diddle diddle: rhyming slang for middle and piddle.

Hide the sausage (play): sexual intercourse. *Bazza's playing hide the sausage with Shazza.*

High as a dingo's howl: fowl smelling.

Hip pocket nerve: a reference to the area where men keep their wallets and the taxpayer's sensitivity to government imposed charges. *The new tax will really hit the hip pocket nerve.*

Hit the hay/sack: go to bed/sleep.

Hit the frog and toad: to hit the road, usually said by a visitor when they are ready to leave.

Hit your kick: open your wallet.

Home and hosed: finished the task well.

Hooks: fingers.

Hooley: a wild party.

Aussie Slang Dictionary

Hoon: a lout or a lair in a (usually loud) car; to drive around with a loud exhaust and a squeal of tires to draw attention to oneself.

Hope your balls turn into bicycle wheels and back pedal up your arse: a colourful curse.

Hooroo: goodbye.

Hooter: nose.

Horizontal exercise/dancing: sexual intercourse.

Horses for courses: fitting the right person to a particular task.

Hotter than a shearer's armpit: unpleasantly hot.

Hottie: hot water bottle.

Hot under the collar: to get angry.

Howzat!: expression used by cricketers when appealing for a batsman to be given out. From *how's that!*

84

Hubby: husband.

Humdinger: something excellent.

Hump a bluey: old term for carrying a swag.

Humping: having sex.

Humpy: a rough-made shack or lean-to in the bush.

Hung like a Mallee bull: well endowed male genitals.

Hungry as a black dog: very hungry; famished.

I

I hope your chooks turn into emus and kick your dunny door down!: An Australian curse.

Iceberg: a die-hard swimmer who goes in the water all year round.

Icy pole: popsicle.

Idiot box: the television.

Iffy: of doubtful merit or risky, perhaps of suspicious origins. *The weather looks* *a bit iffy. The plan sounds iffy to me.*

If he laughed, his face would fall off, or crack: a dreary/very gloomy person.

If his brains were dynamite they wouldn't blow his hat off: refers to someone with limited intelligence.

If it was raining palaces, I'd be hit on the head by a dunny door: I'm about as unlucky as you can get.

Ikey: a Jew. Refers to an early Tasmanian convict named Ikey Solomon, the Fagan of Dickens fame. Also can mean miserly, ungenerous. *My grandfather's real ikey.*

I'll be buggered: an expression of surprise or amazement.

I'll be a monkey's uncle: an expression of surprise.

Illywhacker: con man.

In a tizz: in a state of confusion or confused excitement.

Aussie Slang Dictionary

In good nick: in good shape; fit and healthy.

In like Flynn: successful.

Innings: life span. Refers to a team's time at the wicket (chance to score) in cricket.

In the cactus: in trouble.

In the club/pudding club: pregnant.

In the nick: in jail.

In ya boot!: I don't agree – so there!

Iron lung (wouldn't work in an): a lazy individual.

Iron out: to knock someone unconscious.

Irrits: to be irritated or annoyed immensely. *She really gives me the irrits.*

Is the Pope a Catholic?: it's true, don't doubt it!

It's a freckle past a hair: a response when someone asks for the time and you're not wearing a watch.

I've seen a better head on a glass of beer: an insulting description of someone you consider to be ugly.

Ivories: your teeth or to the play the piano. *He sure can tickle the ivories.*

J

Jackass: kookaburra.

Jack of: tired of. *I got jack of her borrowing my car.*

Jack of all trades: someone who is good at a bit of everything.

Jack of all trades, master of none: a person that will try anything.

Aussie Slang Dictionary

Jack and jill (i will fix your): to pay the bill.

Jackaroo: young drover/stockman in training on a country station.

Jack/jimmy dancer: cancer.

Jack up: to refuse to do something.

Jaffle: toasted sandwich with sealed edges.

Jam jars: thick lensed spectacles.

Jarrah jerker: a Western Australian timber worker.

Jeeze: exclamation. Refers to Jesus.

Jerry: pot under the bed that you urinate in at night.

Jesus wept!: an exclamation.

Jiffy: a moment; short space of time.

Jiggered: broken, useless or doesn't work.

Jillaroo: female jackaroo.

Jimmy riddle: rhyming slang for piddle.

Jimmy Woodser: solitary drink or a lone drinker.

Jocks: male underpants.

Joe Blake: rhyming slang for snake.

Joe Bloggs: average guy.

Joe Blow: average bloke.

Joey: baby kangaroo.

Johnny cake: a type of damper.

Journo: journalist.

Jumbuck: merino sheep.

Jumper: sweater or jersey.

Jungle juice: home made booze.

K

Kangaroo hop: the jerky driving of a learner who cannot control the clutch.

Kangaroos loose in the top paddock: an individual who is a bit mad.

Kark it: to die.

Keen as mustard: enthusiastic.

Keep one for ron: keep something in reserve (for later on).

Kelpie: Australian sheepdog.

Kerfuffle: ado, fuss and bother.

Khyber Pass: rhyming slang for arse.

Kick a goal: to have sexual intercourse.

Kick in: to donate to a whip around at the office or social club.

Kiddiewink: child.

Kindy: kindergarten.

King ping: leading figure.

Kip: a brief nap.

Kiss my arse!: exclamation of disbelief.

Kite flyer: a person who passes discredited cheques.

Kiwi: New Zealander.

Knackered: exhausted.

Aussie Slang Dictionary

Knee high to a grasshopper: someone short in size/stature.

Knickers: female underwear.

Knock: to criticise or have sexual intercourse.

Knock the dags off a sick canary (couldn't): a person with no strength of effectiveness.

Knockback: a rebuttal or refusal. *He got a knockback from the girl he proposed to.*

Knocked up: pregnant.

Knockers: people who criticise; a woman's breasts.

Knock-off time: the end of the working day.

Knock-shop: a brothel.

Knotted (get): go away.

Know a thing or two: to be well versed in matters, particularly of a sexual nature.

Know if a tram was up him unless the conductor rang the bell (wouldn't): refers to a person who doesn't know what's going on.

Knuckle sandwich: a punch in the mouth.

Aussie Slang Dictionary

L

La-de-da: fancy, posh or affecting superior manners.

Lady blamey: a beer glass made from the bottom half of a beer bottle.

Lady's waist: a gracefully shaped beer glass.

Lag: inform, dob.

Lair: a lout who also dresses in a flashy manner.

Lairise around: to behave in a boorish manner to draw attention to yourself.

Lame-brained: someone that is stupid.

Lamington: a small cube of sponge cake, dipped in chocolate and rolled in coconut.

Lamington drive: a fund raising effort.

Larrikin: a likeable lout.

Larry Dooley: mayhem; confusion.

Land shark: a property developer.

Lashing out: going on a spending spree or getting violent/angry.

Laugh at the lawn: to vomit outside.

Lav: abbreviation of lavatory (toilet).

Lead you up the garden path: to lead you astray.

Leak (to take a): urinate.

Aussie Slang Dictionary

Leckie: electrician.

Leftie: socialist or communist.

Legal eagle: a lawyer or solicitor.

Leg opener: an alcoholic beverage offered with the intention of reducing a woman's sexual inhibition.

Leg pull: a trick or hoax.

Lemon: something faulty right from the start that leaves a sour taste in your mouth.

Lezzo: lesbian.

Lie doggo: to remain hidden; to avoid work.

Lift doesn't go all the way to the top floor (the): refers to someone who is mentally deficient.

Lights are on but nobody's home: said of a dim wit.

Like a bad smell: an unwanted presence.

Like a possum up a gum tree: totally at home, very happy.

Like a one-legged man at an arse-kicking party: out of place; ill at ease.

Like a shag on a rock: lonely; to stand out in a crowd.

Like a stunned mullet: astounded; immobilised by surprise.

Like a two-bob watch: crazy; erratic. Refers to a cheap time piece in the old currency.

Like billyo: energetically; with great gusto.

Like putting marshmallow into a money box: refers to the difficulty of inserting a less than erect penis into a vagina.

Like the clappers: fast. *That old car still goes like the clappers.*

Like two ferrets fighting in a sack: refers to a woman's large wobbly backside.

Like watching paint dry: refers to a boring event or spectacle.

Lippy: lipstick.

Liquid amber: beer.

Liquid laugh: vomit.

Liquid lunch: midday meal of beer and more beer.

Little beauty/little ripper: a person or thing of excellence.

Little Vegemites: children.

Little boys: saveloys, cocktail sausages.

Little house: an outdoor toilet.

Lit up like a Manly ferry: intoxicated; drunk.

Lively as a blow fly on a winter's day: lethargic.

Living the life of Riley: to live a carefree, luxurious life.

Loaded: very drunk or very wealthy.

Lob in/lob up: to turn up unexpectedly.

Local bike: promiscuous woman.

Local yokel: a well known resident; someone who lives locally.

Lofty: a tall person.

Lolly: a sweet or candy.

Lolly (do your): lose your temper.

Lolly water: watery, sweet drink with or without alcohol.

Long drink of water: someone very tall.

Aussie Slang Dictionary

Long neck: large bottle of beer (750mL).

Long paddock: a farmer's term for the grassy land beside the road.

Loo: toilet.

Look like death warmed up: to look very ill.

Looks like an unmade bed: untidily dressed.

Looney bin: mental institution.

Lord or Lady Muck: someone who looks down on others. *Who does she think she is, Lady Muck?*

Lousy: ill or disappointingly poor. *I feel lousy. The dinner was lousy.*

Lousy Bastard: an individual who won't loan money to a friend; a tightwad.

Low as a shark: despicable.

Lower than a snake's belly: the lowest of the low kind of person.

Lucked out: to have bad luck.

Lucky Country: Australia.

Lucky as a bastard on Father's Day: unlucky

Lumbered: to be left with responsibility for something, such as a restaurant bill or rubbish.

Lunatic soup: cheap red wine.

Lurk: a good deal. *She's on a good lurk in that job.*

Lyre bird: a compulsive liar.

M

Mad as a cut snake: insane, crazy and dangerous.

Mad as a gumtree full of galahs: mentally unbalanced; insane.

Mad as a meat axe: crazy.

Maggoty: angry; furious.

Magpie: hoarder.

Mainlanders: this is how Tasmanians refer to their fellow Australian who don't live on their island.

M

Make a proper galah of yourself: to look an idiot; make a fool of yourself.

Make a quid: to earn a living.

Man in white: the umpire in an Aussie Rules Football game.

Map of (mappa) Tassie: a woman's pubic hair.

Mate: most common form of address, friend.

Mateship: friends sticking together and helping each other out.

Mate's rates: special deals for friends.

Matildas: old term for a swag or rolled up blanket.

Mean as bird shit: tight fisted; not willing to depart with money.

Mexican: a southerner or Victorian (south of the N.S.W. border).

Mick: Roman Catholic.

Mickey (taking the): sending someone up; deflating their ego.

Middle of nowhere: in the outback.

Middy: a 285 ml glass of beer.

Miffed: mildly annoyed.

Milk bar: corner store; small general produce shop.

Mingy: mean; stingy.

Min min: mythical or mysterious lights in the outback.

Missus: wife.

Mediterranean back: back injuries leading to workers' compensation claim. Refers to the alleged prevalence of this condition among migrants.

Mob: group of people; herd of kangaroos.

Mockers: to put the mockers on

someone is to jinx them.

Moke: a horse or donkey.

Moleskin squatter: a working man that has saved enough cash to buy a small sheep farm.

Molly dook/molly dooker: left handed person.

Mondayitis: aversion to going back to work on Monday.

Mongrel: a terrible person; dog of mixed breed.

Monkey suit: formal dinner suit.

Month of Sundays: a long time. *We haven't seen him in a month of Sundays.*

Moosh: your mouth.

Mopoke: a boring person.

More arse than class: more luck than style.

Aussie Slang Dictionary

More front than Myers (or David Jones): bold, cheeky, not backward at putting yourself forward!

More movements than a Swiss watch: refers to a shifty devious person.

More than you can poke a stick at: a lot.

Morning glory: the erection a bloke wakes up with in the morning.

Mousetraps in his pockets: a miserly individual.

Mouthful of marbles: plummy or incoherent speech.

Mozzie: mosquito.

Muck about: waste time fooling around.

Mug: a fool; a person easily duped; a person's face.

Mug's game: a situation or activity that brings more trouble than reward.

Mulga (gone up to): gone bush.

Mulga madness: going insane after spending time alone in the outback.

Mundee: Monday.

Munga: food.

Muso: abbreviated form of musician.

Mystery bag: rhyming slang for a snag (a sausage).

My stomach thinks my throat's cut: I'm very hungry.

Myxo: myxomatosis, a rabbit disease created by the CSIRO to destroy Australia's plague of rabbits in the fifties.

N

Nana: banana.

Nappies: diapers.

Nark: an individual who spoils another's enjoyment or pesters and annoys.

Nasho: national service, no longer compulsory.

Nasty piece of work: an unpleasant person.

NCR rating: Number of Cans Required. The number of beers you need to drink before you would consider having sex with someone.

Needie: a horse.

Nelly: cheap wine.

Never-never: the outback of the outback; buying goods on credit.

We'll pay for the Rolls Royce on the never-never.

Nick (in the): naked; in the nude.

Nicked: to have stolen something, or to be arrested. *I nicked a CD and then they called the cops and I got nicked.*

Nick off!: go away, now!

Nick off: to sneak away when you are supposed to stay.

Nineteenth hole: the bar at the golf club.

Ning-nong: Or just plain nong. A dill; a dim wit.

Nipper: young surf lifesaver.

Nippy: chilly.

Noah's ark: rhyming slang for shark.

Noggin: skull.

Non-compos: insensible; unconscious.

Aussie Slang Dictionary

From the Latin phrase: *non compos mentis.*

No drama: not a problem.

No hoper: a loser.

Norks: a woman's breasts.

Nose down, bum up: very busy; hard at work.

Nose, on the: smells bad; is dubious.

Nosh up: a large meal.

Not much chop: not very good.

Not a patch on: not as good as something else.

Not an earthly: no chance or no idea.

Not backward in coming forward: a brash person; rude.

Nothing between the ears: stupid.

Not the full quid: mentally deficient;

something missing up top.

Not the sharpest knife in the cutlery drawer: refers to a slow or dull individual.

Not the sharpest tool in the shed: refers to the same unintelligent person as above.

Not what it's cracked up to be: a disappointing standard; not equal to its reputation.

No worries: no problem; she'll be right.

No wukkin' furries: a deliberate spoonerism on no F***ing worries.

Nuddy (in the): totally naked.

Nude nut: a bald person.

Nuggety: small but tough.

Nuggets: testicles.

Nulla-nulla: Aboriginal heavy wooden club.

Ocker: uncouth, uncultured loud mouth, the Down Under representative at the Annual Redneck Awards.

Off one's face: drunk.

Off the beaten track: on a road not used very often.

Off like a bride's nightie: to leave very quickly.

Off like a bucket of prawns in the hot sun: something that stinks.

Off like a robber's dog: to depart quickly.

Off-sider: assistant or partner.

Off your tucker: to have no appetite.

Old chook: a silly old woman.

Old crackers: elderly people.

Old fella: penis.

Olds: parents.

On a good wicket: doing well without too much effort.

On a sticky wicket: in trouble.

On the blink: not working reliably; about to break down.

On the bugle/nose: foul smelling.

On the make: seeking sexual conquest.

On the Murray cod: rhyming slang for on the nod; on credit.

On the outer: a pariah; to be rejected socially.

On the tin roof: something provided free of charge by the management.

On the turps: drinking heavily.

Aussie Slang Dictionary

On the wagon: abstaining from alcohol.

On the wallaby track: travelling in the outback.

On the wrong tram: to be following a wrong train of thought; to misunderstand an issue.

On your Pat Malone: rhyming slang for on your own.

Once over (give it the): to check something thoroughly.

One-armed bandit: poker machine.

One up against your duckhouse: a set-back.

Onkaparinga: brand of woollen blanket; rhyming slang for finger.

Onya!: good on you.

Ooroo!: goodbye.

Open slather: open to all comers; no restraints.

Optic nerve: rhyming slang for perve.

Op shop: opportunity shop, where second hand goods are sold.

Order of the boot: to be given the (Royal) order of the boot is to be fired from your job.

Organise a fart in a bean factory (couldn't): refers to someone who has no organisational skills whatsoever.

Organise a piss in a brewery (couldn't): refers to the same useless individual as above.

Organise a shit fight in a septic tank: the same disorganised person as above!

O.S.: overseas.

Out for lunch: lacking in intelligence or concentration.

Aussie Slang Dictionary

Out of the box: exceptionally good; very special.

Out to grass: retired.

Out to it/out of it: totally drunk.

Outback: the desert heart of the continent, hot, remote and unhospitable country.

Outlaws: in-laws.

Oxford/Rhodes scholar: rhyming slang for dollar.

Oz: shorthand for Australia.

P

Pack of galahs: group of idiots.

Pack/cack your dacks: to be terrified.

Panic merchant: an individual who panics easily and tries to spread that panic.

Paper yabber: letter.

Paralytic: very drunk and unable to stand.

Park a tiger on the rug: to vomit.

Parrot mouth: a talkative person.

Paron's nose: the fatty nose-shaped end of a roast chicken.

Pash: a passionate kiss.

Pash on: behave in a passionate, sexual way with someone.

Pass over the Great Divide: to expire; to end.

Pat Malone: you are on your own/ alone.

Pav: short for pavlova, a meringue dessert.

Paw-paw: Queensland papaya (tropical fruit).

Pay through the nose: to part with too much cash; to pay more than something is worth.

Pearl: excellent.

Penguin: a nun.

Perk: a freebie; something for nothing that comes with your job; to vomit.

Perve: short for pervert; to ogle. *Come and have a perve at these norks, Bazza.*

Pester: annoy or bother someone.

Pick/pull the skin off a rice-pudding: refers to a weak or ineffectual person.

Piece of cake: an easy task.

Pie-eater: South Australian.

Piffle: nonsense.

Pig's bum: that's wrong; incorrect.

Pike out: to reneg on a deal or arrangement.

Piker: an individual who gives up or quits too easily.

Pinch: arrest.

Pint: large glass of beer, especially in South Australia.

Pipped at the post: narrowly beaten.

Piss: urine; to urinate; alcohol.

Pissed as a newt/parrot: drunk.

Pissed off: very annoyed.

Piss in someone's pocket: to crawl, or ingratiate yourself with someone.

Piss in the wind: to behave ineffectually.

Piss on you if you were on fire (wouldn't): refers to a mean person.

Pisspot: a heavy drinker.

Piss up: a party.

Plate of meat: your feet.

Play funny buggers: attempt to deceive.

Play possum: to pretend to be asleep.

Play the neddies: to gamble on horses.

Plonk: cheap wine.

Plum pud: rhyming slang for good.

Poddy dodger: cattle rustler.

Point Percy at the porcelain: to urinate in the toilet bowl.

P

Point the bone at: to predict failure; to blame someone.

Poison shop: a licensed hotel or bottle shop.

Poke in the eye with a sharp stick (better than): the situation is not ideal, but you will make the most of it.

Pokies: poker machines.

Pommie/Pom: an English person. Refers to Prisoner of Her Majesty, or Prisoner of mother England.

Pong: stink.

Poofter/poof: homosexual male.

Poohie: in a bad mood.

Pooned up: well dressed.

Possum: a loving nick or pet name.

Possum guts: a coward.

Postie: postman.

123

Aussie Slang Dictionary

Possie: position; seating place.

Posh: well bred and very wealthy.

Pot: 285ml beer glass in Queensland and Victoria.

Pot calling the kettle black: someone said something adverse about you and you reply with this phrase (which says that they are the same or worse).

Pot hole: hole in the road.

Poxie/poxy: small, rubbishy and of poor quality.

Pozzie: position.

Prang: a minor car accident.

Prawn: shrimp.

Preggers: pregnant.

Pressies: gifts, presents.

Proddy-dog/prodhopper: old derogatory term used by Catholics or Protestants.

Proud as a rat with a gold tooth: someone who is very proud of how they look or something they have done.

Puffed: out of breath.

Pull a swifty: to trick someone.

Pull someone's leg: to play a trick on someone.

Pull the other one: I don't believe you!

Pull up your socks: get your life in order; get your act together.

Pull your head in mate: tell someone to mind their own business.

Pure merino: first class; excellent quality.

Purler: something that is great or excellent.

Purple patch: a run of good luck.

Push-bike: bicycle.

Push shit uphill with a sharp stick: to engage in a hopeless, impossible task.

Put a cork/sock in it!: shut up!

Put the bite on: to ask for a loan of money. *Davo put the bite on me for fifty bucks.*

Put the boot in: to attack someone when they are down.

Put the hard word on: to pressure someone.

Put the mockers on: to jinx or frustrate someone.

Put up job: a deceptive or contrived situation.

Put up your dooks!: to challenge someone to a fight.

Qantas: originally Queensland and Northern Territory Air Service. The well-known Australian Airline with the flying red kangaroo as its emblem.

Quack: a doctor. *I felt crook so I went to the quack.*

Quaky Isles: New Zealand.

Quandong: a person who lives off others.

Quick snort: a rushed drink of alcohol.

Quid: former slang term for Australian pound which was superceded in the sixties by the dollar.

R

Rabbit: to tackle another player around the ankles (in football).

Rabbit killer: to hit someone on the back of the neck with the side of your hand.

Rabbit on: to natter mindlessly.

Racecourse emu: a punter who searches the racecourse grounds for discarded winning tickets.

Racing off: to have sex with someone else's wife or husband.

Rack off: get lost! *Rack off, Johnno!*

Rafferty's rules: a free for all; no holds barred.

Rag (the): newspaper; a woman who sleeps around.

Rage: party.

Raincoat: sometimes means a condom, depending on the context.

Raining cats and dogs: heavy rain/ storm.

Randy as mallee bull: sexually aroused.

Rank: stinks.

Rapt: to be very pleased with. *She was rapt with her present.*

Rare as rocking horse shit: very rare.

Ratbag: a scallywag, brat.

Rat shit/R.S.: no good.

Rattle your dags!: get a move on.

Ratty: snarky and unpredictable.

Reckon: to guess or estimate.

Reg Grundies: undies. Refers to a well-known former TV producer.

Aussie Slang Dictionary

Rego: car registration.

Rellies: relatives.

Rhodes scholar: a top student; rhyming slang for dollar.

Richard Cranium: fancy way of saying Dick Head, which means idiot.

Ridgie-didge: the real thing; authentic.

Ring: centre of operations at a two-up school; backside.

Ringer: the fastest shearer in the shearing shed.

Ring-in: substitute, usually a last-minute arrangement.

Ripe (smells): smells off or bad.

Rip off: cheated.

Ripper: fantastic.

Ripper (you little): exclamation of delight.

Ripsnorter: excellent.

Road train: long haul, multi-wheel base vehicle usually encountered on remote highways.

Roam around like a lost sheep: to wander aimlessly or to be lost.

Roaring trade (doing a): doing a lot of business.

Roar the tripe out of: to give a dressing-down; to verbally abuse.

Rock, the: Uluru or Ayers Rock, the monolith in the Northern Territory.

Rock up: to turn up; to arrive. *Let's rock up to the pub at 11.*

Rollie: a hand-rolled cigarette.

Rolls canardly: a bomby car (it rolls down hills and can hardly get up them).

Roo: kangaroo.

Roo bar: large metal frame on the front of a vehicle for deflecting kangaroos in the bush. Also known as a bull bar.

Root: sexual intercourse.

Rooted: tired.

Ropable: very angry.

Rort: a rip off; a dodgy scheme.

Rotgut: awful cheap wine that feels like it's eating your stomach.

Rough as bags/rough as a pig's breakfast: uncouth; rude; lacking in finesse.

Rough end of the pineapple/stick: the poor end of a deal.

Rough nut: unsophisticated person.

Rough up: a noisy brawl.

Rouseabout: an odd job man.

Rubbity dub: rhyming slang for pub.

Ruby dazzler: an excellent person or thing.

Rugger bugger: a macho footballer.

Rug rats: children; babies.

Rug up: to dress warmly for cold weather.

Run about like a chook with its head cut off: to race around pointlessly.

Run around in the shower to get wet (have to): refers to a very thin person.

Run dead: to deliberately lose a race.

Run-in: argument.

Run like a hairy goat: to perform badly in a race.

Run like stink: to run fast.

Run of outs: to have a losing streak.

Run the rabbit: to obtain alcohol after hours.

Rush your fences: to act without thinking.

Rustbucket: a bomb of a car.

Rybuck: good; excellent.

Rybuck shearer: an expert shearer.

S

Sacked: fired from work.

Salvo: member of the Salvation Army.

Same diff: no difference, virtually the same thing.

Same here!: an expression of agreement.

Sammie: a sandwich.

Sandgroper: Western Australian.

Sandshoes: joggers, sneakers, trainers.

Sandwich short of a picnic: not quite all there mentally.

Sandy blight: an eye problem common in the outback caused by dust getting in the eyes.

Sandy McNab: rhyming slang for cab.

Aussie Slang Dictionary

Sanga/er: sandwich.

Satdee: Saturday.

Sausage short of a barbecue: a dumb individual.

Scarce as hen's teeth: something extremely rare.

School at Christmas (like): has no class.

Schooner: a large beer glass in NSW and Qld, but a small beer glass in South Australia!

Scorcher: a very hot day; a very sexy date.

Scratchy: instant lottery ticket.

Scrub: bushland.

Scrubbers: wild cattle; promiscuous women.

Scrub-up well: to look good in formal or semi-formal wear.

136

Scumbag: a person of low morals.

Scunge: an individual who is derelict, unwashed and smells bad. Or to borrow (and normally not repay) a small amount of money or goods from someone.

Scungy: mean; a miserable portion.

See ya later: goodbye.

Seen his/her last gumtree: on the verge of death.

Sell ice to the Eskimos: the ability to sell anything to anyone, in particular things they do not need.

Selling tickets on himself/herself: a conceited, arrogant person.

Aussie Slang Dictionary

Semi: semi trailer.

Septic tank: rhyming slang for Yank.

Servo: service station.

Settler's clock: kookaburra.

Shack: a crude kind of house or country cottage.

Shag: sexual intercourse.

Shaggin' wagon: panel van used for sexual exploits.

Shaky Isles: New Zealand.

Shank's pony: to travel on foot.

Sharkbait: someone who swims out beyond all the other swimmers at the beach.

Shark biscuit: somebody new to surfing.

Shearer's joy: beer.

Sheila: girl or woman.

S

She'll be right, mate: an assurance that things will work out.

Shepherd's friend: dingo.

Sherbert: beer.

Shickered: totally drunk.

Shifter/shifter brains: a stupid person.

Shindig: noisy party.

Shiny arse: public servant or politician.

Shiralee: swag (a rolled up blanket).

Shirty: short tempered; easily crossed.

Shit hot: very impressive.

Shit house: poor quality, unenjoyable. *The footy was shit house.* Also refers to a toilet.

Shit shoveller: menial labourer.

Shivoo: a wild party.

Aussie Slang Dictionary

Shonky: dodgy, doubtful, unreliable.

Shook on: aroused by.

Shoot through: to leave suddenly to avoid paying a debt.

Short arms and deep pockets: an individual who will not part with their money, or won't buy a round when it's their turn.

Short and curlies: refers to pubic hair. To be held by the short and curlies is to be in a dire predicament.

Short arse: a short person.

Short of numbers in the Upper House: stupid.

Shot full of holes: very drunk.

Shot through like a Bondi tram: departed hastily.

Shout: to pay for a round of drinks.

Shouse: short for shit house, or toilet.

140

Shovel shit: to work in a menial job.

Sickie: day off work.

Silly as a two bob watch: to act crazy.

Silly sausage: a term usually applied to small children when they are being silly.

Silvertail: privileged member of the wealthy class.

Sin bin: a panel van fitted out for entertaining females and enjoying their favours.

Since Cocky was an egg: a long time ago.

Singlet: a tanktop; sleeveless undershirt.

Sink a few: to have a few drinks.

Sinker: a meat pie.

Sink the boot in: to kick someone violently; to attack verbally.

Sink the sav/sink the sausage: sexual

intercourse.

Sink the slipper: to kick during a fight.

Siphon the python: to urinate.

Sitting on an ant's nest: in a situation that is about to get worse.

Skedaddle: to leave in a hurry.

Skerrick: a very tiny portion; a smidgeon.

Skew-whiff: all awry; out of order.

Skinful: drunk.

Skinny as a sapling with the bark scraped off: very thin.

Skint: penniless.

Skite: braggart or show off.

Skittle: to knock something down.

Skull: to drink a whole bottle or glass of alcohol in one go, without taking a breath.

Sky pilot: clergyman.

Slab: a pack of 24 cans of beer.

Slacker: a lazy person.

Slag: a loose woman.

Slag off at: to pour contempt on.

Sleepout: closed in-house verandah, for extra bedroom.

Slow as a wet week in a caravan: painfully slow.

Sly grog: illegal alcohol.

Smack a blue: to strike trouble; get into a fight.

Smackers/smackeroos: money/dollars.

Smashed: drunk.

Smoko: a short break from work in which to smoke a cigarette.

Snag: sausage.

Aussie Slang Dictionary

Snagger: a 'learner' shearer.

Snag short of a barbie: lacking in intelligence.

Snake juice: strong alcohol.

Snake's hiss: rhyming slang for piss.

Snaky: in a vile mood.

Snarler: sausage.

Snog: a passionate kiss.

Snow/snowy: nickname for a blonde or white haired person.

Snowdrop: to steal clothes from a washing line.

So low he could parachute out of the belly of a snake: refers to a person of low moral character.

So low he gets upgraded to economy class: refers to a person of low moral character.

So poor he/she woudl lick paint off the fence: very poor.

So slow he/she couldn't get a job as a speed hump: lethargic; slow witted.

So wet you could shoot ducks off him/her: idiotic.

Sook/sookybub: a wimp, someone who bursts into tears easily.

Soup strainer: a moustache.

Southerly Buster: a cool wind that blows up in Sydney after a hot spell.

Spag bol: spaghetti bolognese.

Sparkie: electrician.

Sparrow's fart: daybreak; first light of morning.

Speak into the big white telephone: to vomit into the lavatory.

Speedos: swim wear, generally men's bathers.

Aussie Slang Dictionary

Speed merchant: a fast car driver.

Speewa: mythical outback location.

Spew: to vomit.

Spewin': very angry. *Stevo was spewin'!*

Spewy: unattractive; awful.

Spinebash: to sleep.

Spit chips: to express frustration.

Spit the dummy: to throw a tantrum. Refers to a baby refusing its pacifier, preferring to scream.

Splash the boots: to urinate.

Sponger: someone who lives off the efforts of others.

Spruiker: a person who touts with a loud hailer for business.

Sprung: caught in the act.

Spud: a potato.

146

Spunk: a sexy or desirable person of either sex.

Squatter: a person living on premises without permission.

Squatter's daughter: rhyming slang for water.

Square up: to set things right, make amends.

Squiz: a hurried look. *Take a squiz at this!*

Stack: to crash a car.

Stack your drapery: to put your coat on the ground before a fight.

Aussie Slang Dictionary

Stands out like a black crow in a bucket of milk: obvious.

Stands/sticks out like a country dunny: immediately obvious.

Starkers: naked.

State election: rhyming slang for erection.

Station: large country property, usually with cattle or sheep grazing.

Steak and Kidney: rhyming slang for Sydney.

Sticks out like a dog's balls: blatantly obvious.

Stick your bib in: to interfere when not asked to.

Sticky tape: adhesive tape, also called Durex.

Sticky beak: a person who is overly curious or (verb) to inspect something closely. *I'll just go take a sticky beak at that new house.*

148

Stiff bickies: too bad.

Stiff cheddar: too bad, I have no sympathy!

Still kicking: alive.

Stingy: mean; ungenerous.

Stinker: a very hot day.

Stinko: smells; drunk.

Stirrer: an individual who deliberately or sometimes playfully causes trouble.

Stir the possum: to raise controversial issues; to create a disturbance.

Stockman: a station worker.

Stoked: extremely happy.

Stonkered: exhausted; drunk.

Stone the crows!: an expression of astonishment or frustration.

Stony/stony broke: penniless; broke.

Storm stick: umbrella.

Stoush: to punch or bash up.

Strain the potatoes: to urinate.

Strapped for cash: short of money; broke.

Stretch: nickname for a tall person.

Strewth!: another expression of surprise. Refers to *God's Truth!*

Strike a light: another expression of astonishment.

Strine: the Australian version of English.

Stroppy lorrakeet parade: general city traffic madness.

Stubbies: short shorts for blokes.

Stubby: a squat bottle of beer.

Stubby holder: polystyrene insulated holder for a stubby bottle or can.

S

Stuck-up: conceited.

Stuffed: very tired; useless and beyond repair.

Stunned: amazed; drunk.

Suck: an obnoxious person.

Sunbake: sunbathe; lie in the sun.

Sunbeam: a piece of crockery or cutlery that has not been used during a meal.

Sunday dog: a lazy person.

Sundowner: a lazy person; an organised get together after work.

Sunnies: sunglasses.

Super: superannuation or retirement pension.

Surfies: surfers.

Suss (a bit): probably of dubious origins; worthy of suspicion.

Suss out: to check something out to make sure it is all above board.

Swag: rolled up bedding as carried by a swagman.

Swaggie/Swagman: tramp; hobo.

Sweat on it: to wait apprehensively.

Sweet Fanny Adams: zilch; none; nothing.

Sword swallower: a person that eats off a knife.

Sydney Harbour: rhyming slang for barber.

Sydneyite: a resident of Sydney.

T

Ta: thanks.

T.A.B: Totalisator Agency Board, government controlled betting shops.

Take the piss out of: to be sarcastic towards.

Take a piece out of: to berate someone; give a piece of your mind.

Take a punt: to take a chance; to make a bet.

Take a shine to: to warm to something; to find a person likeable.

Take the mickey out of: to tease or ridicule someone.

Tall poppies: successful people.

Tall poppy syndrome: to criticise successful people.

Aussie Slang Dictionary

Tally: to keep score.

Talk the lid off an iron pot: someone who talks a lot.

Talk under wet cement (can): refers to a person who never stops chattering.

Tanked: drunk.

Tart up: to do a superficial makeover.

Take a piece out of: to berate.

Tassie Tiger: someone from Tasmania.

Taswegian: a Tasmanian.

Tatty: ragged; shabby.

Technicolour yawn: vomit.

Tee up: to arrange something.

Telly: television.

Ten ounce sandwich: lunch consisting of only beer.

That's the way the Violet Crumbles: an observation on the way things have turned out. Refers to a honeycomb chocolate bar that shatters easily.

Thick as a brick: dull; slow witted.

Thick as two planks: not very bright; unintelligent.

Thingamajig: term used when you can't remember the real name.

Things are crook in Tallarook: times are pretty bad.

Thinks the sun shines out of his/her arse: to have high regard, usually exaggerated, for someone.

Thongs: rubber sandals (flip flops) with straps only between the first and second toes, usually worn to the beach.

Three parts gone: inebriated.

Throw your voice: to vomit.

Aussie Slang Dictionary

Thunder box: outdoor toilet.

Thursdee: Thursday.

Tick: short period of time. *I'll be there in a tick (of the clock).*

Ticker: the heart.

Tickets on oneself (to have): to think you're great.

Tickle the till: to rob someone or a business.

Tide's gone out (the): your glass needs a refill.

Tighter than a fish's bumhole: a scrooge or miser.

Tin ear: an eavesdropper.

Tin lid: child; rhyming slang for kid.

Tinny: a can of beer; referring to someone who is uncannily lucky.

Tip the finger: to drink alcohol.

To go to town: to go hammer and tongs; to berate someone.

To have the trots: to suffer from diarrhoea; to have tickets on yourself: to be vain and conceited.

Toey: short tempered; impatient.

Togs: swimming costume.

Top End: Northern Territory.

Top Ender: Northern Territorian.

Too right!: definitely.

Tough as fencing wire: very rough.

Trackie daks/trackies: tracksuit pants.

Train choko vine over a country dunny (can't): refers to an ineffectual or weak person.

Trap for young players: a problem for novices or the unaware.

Trifecta: events that happen in threes, similar to a hat trick.

Aussie Slang Dictionary

Trimmer: an excellent person or thing.

Triple fronted brick vanilla/venereal: cream brick dream home of the sixties.

Trooper: policeman.

Troppo: gone mad.

Trots: diarrhoea.

Trouble and strife: rhyming slang for wife.

Truckie: truck driver.

True blue: genuine.

Trunks: swimming shorts.

Tubes: large cans of beer.

Tucker: food.

Tucker bag: food bag.

Tucker chute: mouth.

Tuckshop: school canteen or cafeteria.

158

Tuesdee: Tuesday.

Tumble to: to become aware of.

Turn dingo: inform on others.

Turn it up!: exclamation of disbelief.

Turn-up for the books (a): a surprising outcome, from racing parlance.

Turps: a strong drink.

Twig: to suddenly comprehend.

Twit: an idiot.

Two pot screamer: a person who gets drunk easily.

Two men and a dog: poor attendance; very few people.

Two-up: an Australian gambling game where two coins are tossed with players betting on heads or tails.

U

Uluru: the Aboriginal and now common name for Ayres Rock.

Umpie: umpire.

Umpteen: a high number. *I've called him umpteen times and he's never home.*

Underdaks: underpants.

Underground mutton: rabbits.

Under the affluence of incahol: drunk.

Under the weather: ill or suffering a hangover.

Undies: underwear.

Unit: a small apartment or flat.

Up shit creek: everything going wrong.

U

Up the donga/donger: out in the country.

Up the duff: pregnant.

Up the gumtree: someone that got them self in a spot of trouble.

Up the pole: confused; incorrect.

Up the spout: ruined or pregnant.

Up yourself: to be conceited.

Up yours!: abusive term.

Up there Cazaly!: call of encouragement, referring to a legendary Australian Rules Footballer.

Useful as an ashtray on a motorbike: no use at all.

Useful as a flywire door on a submarine: useless.

Useful as a one legged man in an arse kicking contest: absolutely useless.

161

Aussie Slang Dictionary

Useless as a handbrake on a Holden: serves no purpose; useless.

Useless as tits on a bull: no use at all.

Ute: utility vehicle, Australian equivalent of a pick-up truck.

Uwie (uee, uie): a u-turn.

V

Vandyke: outdoor lavatory

Veggies: vegetables.

Veggo: vegetarian.

Vee dub: a Volkswagen car.

Vegemite: an Australian vegetable yeast extract spread for bread and biscuits.

Veg out: to rest and relax.

162

Verandah above the toyshop: a large belly on a man.

Verbal diarrhoea: never-ending blather.

Village bike: a promiscuous woman.

Vino: cheap wine.

Visiting card: an article of clothing or object recognisable as belonging to a certain person.

Volcanoes: pimples or boils.

Vulture: a driver that double parks; someone that hangs over another's shoulder while waiting for something.

W

WACA: (pronounced whacker) acronym for the Western Australian Cricket Association and the Perth cricket ground.

Wacker: a crazy person.

Waffle: to talk nonsense.

Wag: to play truant from school.

Wake up Australia!: said to someone daydreaming or not concentrating.

Walkabout: the practice of going bush for an unscheduled time away.

Walkabout (gone): lost.

Walking ticket: to get laid off from your job.

Walkover: something that is done easily or someone deceived easily.

W

Wallaby track: to go on this track is to go wandering in search of a job.

Walloper: a policeman.

Wally: an idiot; someone that forgot something.

Wally Grout: rhyming slang for shout.

Waltzing Matilda: to carry a swag, also a famous Australian song.

Wank: to masturbate.

Wanker: someone who is obviously in love with themself.

Waterhole: the local pub.

Water the horse: to urinate.

Weak as a wet whistle: very weak.

Weak as piss: without strength; having no substance.

Weatherboard: wooden house.

Aussie Slang Dictionary

Wedding tackle: penis.

Weed: tobacco but now more commonly used for marijuana.

Wee wee: pee pee.

Were you born in a tent?: said to someone who continually leaves the door open.

Wellies: Wellington boots; gum boots; waterproof boots.

Well under: drunk.

Welsh on: inform on someone; to fail to pay debts; to betray.

Went through like a dose of salts: to leave quickly.

Westie: someone from the Western suburbs.

Wet (the): monsoon season in the tropical north.

Wet as water: ineffective.

Wet enough to bog a duck: extremely wet weather.

Whacko!: excellent!

Wharfie: waterside worker.

What do you do for a crust?: what do you do for a job?

What's the damage: how much do i owe you?

What's your beef?: what's your problem?

Wheelie: the noisy practice of spinning the wheels of a car by accelerating suddenly.

When the eagle shits: pay day.

When the shit hits the fan: when a problem occurs.

Whinger: a whiner; complainer.

Whinging pom: a complaining English immigrant.

Aussie Slang Dictionary

Whippersnapper: a child; a cheeky young person.

Whirl (give it a): give it a go.

White-ant: to attempt to ruin another's chances. *He white-anted the proposal.*

White pointer: highway patrol.

White pointers: lady sunbaking topless.

Whiz (to take a): urinate.

Whizzer: penis.

Whoopydoo!: an exclamation of delight, but sometimes sarcastic.

Whopper: something enormous.

Who's robbing this coach?: said when someone is interfering.

Why keep a dog and bark yourself?: said to someone that does a task that someone else should do.

Widgie: a female 'bodgie'.

W

Wig-wam/wing-wong for a goose's bridle: frustrated parents' explanation to a persistently questioning child. *And what's that, Daddy? It's a wig-wam for a goose's bridle, son.*

Willies: anxieties, apprehension. *That bloke gives me the willies.*

Willy: penis.

Willy-willy: small dusty whirlwind.

Windy enough to blow a blue dog off its chain: extremely windy.

Within cooee: near, close. Refers to a traditional bush call for help when lost (coo-ee!). *I came within a cooee of winning that prize.*

Wobbly (to chuck a): to throw a tantrum. Similar to *chuck a spaz*.

Wog: a stomach virus; fly larvae; souther European native.

Wombat: refers to a male Casanova. A wombat is a native Australian animal.

169

Wonky: unsteady on the feet.

Won't have a bar of: refuses to have anything to do with, rejects.

Wooden spoon: the award for coming last in the sports table.

Wool chaser: a dog that bites sheep.

Woolloomooloo uppercut: a kick to the groin.

Woolly woofter: rhymes with poofter, which is a term for a male homosexual.

Woop-woop: any remote location.

Woop-woop pigeon: a kookaburra.

Would bet on two flies crawling up a wall: refers to a compulsive gambler.

Would knock your socks off: something amazing.

Would talk a glass eye to sleep: a boring person.

Wouldn't give you the time of day: an uncooperative person.

Wouldn't it rot your socks off!: something very annoying or disgusting.

Wouldn't know him if I found him in my Cornflakes packet: a complete stranger.

Wouldn't know his arse from his elbow: a stupid individual.

Wouldn't know if he was Arthur or Martha: an idiot; someone so drunk they don't know where they are.

Wouldn't shout in a shark attack: a selfish person.

Wouldn't touch with a ten-foot pole: will have nothing to do with it.

Wouldn't use him/her for sharkbait: to hold someone in very low regard.

Wouldn't work in an iron lung: a very lazy individual.

Wowser: killjoy, spoilsport, anti-drinking, anti-fun individual.

Write-off: a car damaged in an accident beyond repair. Refers to the insurance company writing the vehicle off as a loss.

XXXX: (pronounced Four X) brand of beer made in Queensland.

Y

Yabber: to natter, to talk.

Yabbie: small fresh water crayfish.

Yacking: talking a lot.

Yahoo: wild larrikin.

Yakka: hard work. Refers to a brand of tough work wear.

Yanking my chain: telling a lie.

Yank tank: a large American car.

Yarn: a story or to have a good talk with someone.

Yellow fever: gold fever; gold prospecting.

Yobbo: uncouth individual; a lair.

Yodel: to vomit.

Yonks: a long time. *I haven't seen him in yonks.*

Yonnie: a small, smooth, flat stone perfect for skimming across the surface of water.

You beaut!/You little beauty!: a jubilant exclamation.

You'd make a blowfly sick: used as an insult.

Your blood's worth bottling: said to someone that has done something excellent or that you admire.

Youse: plural of you.

Yowie: mythical creature. Like big foot or a yeti.

Z

Zs (catch some): sleep.

Zack: sixpence (pre-decimal equivalent to 5 cents).

Zebra crossing: striped lines across a road, indicating where pedestrians can cross.

Ziff: a beard.

Zilch: zero, nothing.

Zonk: a fool.

Zonked: exhausted, totally worn out.

Also available from Brolga Publishing

A Bushie's Guide to Life!

by Digger Cobber Mate
illustrated by Peter Broelman
ISBN 9780909608064 $12.95

Pithy, wicked, honest, no-nonsense and full of humour, *A Bushie's Guide to Life* captures the essence of the Australian approach to life.

Full of advice from the burning heart of Australia, it still has resonance and validity in the urban centres of the population, reminding us all of what it truly means to be Australian. While giving us a giggle at the same time.

ORDER

Aussie Slang Dictionary
by Lolla Stewart

ISBN 9781922036308   Qty

RRP AU $17.99   .....

Postage within Australia   AU $5.00   .....

TOTAL★ $_____ ★ All prices include GST

Name: ....Phone:...

Address: ....

Email: ....

Payment: ❏ Money Order ❏ Cheque ❏ Amex ❏ MasterCard ❏ Visa

Cardholder's Name:...

Credit Card Number: __ __ __ ___ __ __ ___ __ __ __ __ __ __

Signature: ....Expiry Date: ....

Allow 10 days for delivery.

Payment to: Brolga Publishing (46 063 962 443)
PO Box 12544
A'Beckett Street, Melbourne, 8006
Victoria, Australia
admin@brolgapublishing.com.au

BE PUBLISHED

Publishing through a successful Australian publisher.
Brolga provides:
- Editorial appraisal
- Cover design
- Typesetting
- Printing
- Author promotion
- National book trade distribution, including sales, marketing and distribution.
- Ebook conversions with distribution, sales and marketing internationally.

For details and inquiries, contact:
Brolga Publishing Pty Ltd
PO Box 12544
A'Beckett St VIC 8006

bepublished@brolgapublishing.com.au
markzocchi@brolgapublishing.com.au
ABN: 46 063 962 443